1595

GREAT ARTISTS

PAUL

GAUGUIN

Maria Siponta De Salvia

ENCHANTED LION BOOKS
New York

Paul Gauguin

Paul Gauguin was born in Paris in 1848. The following year his family moved to Peru, but he returned to France at the age of seven to go to school, first in Orleans and then in Paris. At the age of seventeen he joined the merchant navy, where he stayed for two years, travelling around the land of his childhood, South America. He joined the stockbroking firm Bertin in Paris at the age of twenty-three and excelled in his dealings on the stock market. In 1873, he married Mette Sophie Gad, a Danish girl with whom he had five children. The marriage fell apart, however, when Gauguin discovered his talent as a painter. After losing his position at Bertin following the stock market crisis of 1892, he abandoned his family to embark on an adventure that would take him far from his Parisian way of life – a journey that started in Brittany and would ultimately end in Polynesia with his death in the Marquesas Islands in 1903. Even though Impressionism had a great influence on his work, he strived to rediscover art's symbolic values, to free painting from its dependence on the material world and to use his imagination to explore a new, spiritual dimension. This would lead to his ultimate rejection of Impressionism. "Art is an abstraction, extract it from nature and the dream of creation will result," he wrote to a friend as early as 1888, defending his "right to risk everything." His innovative approach to art prepared the way for the Fauves and Expressionists.

Gauguin painted *Interior of the Artist's House, Rue Carcel* while he was in Paris. He alternated between his lucrative work as a stockbroker and the study of drawing. He attended exhibitions assiduously, particularly those of the Impressionists (to whom he had

been introduced by the painter Camille Pissarro), and he started to collect their works. Later he met Cézanne and Degas, who would both have an influence on his style. In 1879, he started to take part in Impressionist exhibitions and achieved some critical success. In the *Interior of the Artist's House, Rue Carcel* Gauguin uses the abbreviated technique of the Impressionists – the little strokes of color that animate the composition, depicting the vibrations of light. The composition of Gauguin's picture also shows the influence of Japanese prints – the decentralized figures and objects, some of which are even cut off at the edges of the canvas.

**Interior of the
Artist's House, Rue
Carcel**
1881, oil on canvas,
51 x 64 in.
(130 x 162 cm.)
Nazjnalgaleriet, Oslo

IN THESE YEARS

1886 Gauguin contributes nineteen works to the last Impressionist

exhibition. His paintings, together with many others on display, show innovative tendencies. **1887** The artist,

recently returned from Pont-Aven in Brittany, leaves in the spring for Panama and Martinique with his friend Laval. This

journey has a great effect on his development as an artist. In November Gauguin is back in Paris, where he meets

Theo and Vincent Van Gogh.

Four Breton Women

Some critics believe that this canvas was painted in 1888. It is more likely, however, to date from Gauguin's first stay at Pont-Aven in Brittany in 1886 (as is suggested by the signature in the lower left of the painting). The painting depicts four Breton women who, according to some, are dancing. However, it also is possible that they are idly passing the time by chatting outside their houses (as is suggested by the woman on the right, who is leaning casually against a wall). Gauguin is clearly attracted to the decorative motif of the woman's white caps, which stand out clearly against both the background and their dark clothing. The "unfinished" Impressionist technique is still visible here, but we can already see the artist's fondness for large areas of color and emphatic outlines. There are strong references here to both to the more "illustrative" and linear paintings of Degas and to the "casual" nature of Japanese prints, where scenes are cut off at the picture's edge.

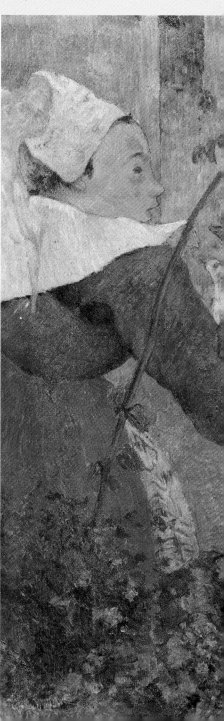

Four Breton Women
1886, oil on canvas, 28¹/₄ x 35³/₄ in. (72 x 91 cm)
Neue Pinakothek, Munich.

THE JAPANESE INFLUENCE

Around the middle of the nineteenth century there was a considerable influx of oriental artefacts into Europe, creating a fashion for *japonaiserie*. Examples of Japanese dress and decoration began to appear in Parisian houses, following the Japanese presence at the Paris *Exposition Universelle* in 1867. Artists became interested in prints and decorated fans from Japan. The influence of Japanese art on European culture was known as "Japonism." Gauguin, too, appears to have succumbed to its fascination.

IN THESE YEARS

1888 Gauguin leaves for Port-Aven in February and before starting to paint

spends time observing and contemplating people and places in order to understand their true character. A new group of

artists, the Nabis (who included Sérusier, Maurice Denis and Bonnard amongst their number) was founded. They followed

Gauguin in his search to "spiritualize" art by simplifying the process of drawing and using intense colors.

Martinique Landscape

This painting is one of the ten that were painted during Gauguin's brief stay in Martinique in 1887. Although he adheres to the Impressionist technique of short brushstrokes and the exploration of parallel hatching developed by Cézanne, Gauguin begins to accentuate the use of color (as his bold depiction of luxuriant tropical vegetation bathed in strong sunlight reveals). Here we start to see his desire to reach beyond visible reality and bestow an indefinable symbolic dimension on his images. The colors are laid on the canvas almost as if in a tapestry in which we can discern the close pattern of the weave. The strokes of thick colour result in an almost entire absence of spatial depth: the vegetation, the sea and the sky seemingly merge into each other. This marks an important step in Gauguin's attempt to negate realism, for which, rightly or wrongly, he blamed the Impressionists.

Martinique Landscape
1887, oil on canvas,
45 x 34³/₄ in.
(115 x 88.5 cm)
*Edinburgh, National
Gallery of Scotland*

THE MARTINIQUE CANVASES

During his four-month stay in Martinique, Gauguin was preoccupied with money matters. Before, in Panama, he had worked as a laborer in order to support himself; in Martinique, he was forced to sell his personal belongings at auction. He raised enough money to secure his passage back to France on a ship and was optimistic that the four canvases he was taking with him would make his fortune in Paris. He was wrong. Even his friends were perplexed by his latest experiments with color. Only Vincent van Gogh understood what Gauguin had been trying to do. It was probably at his suggestion that Theo van Gogh, who worked in a gallery in Paris, took some of his canvases.

Under the Mangoes

The signature – "P. Gauguin '87" – on the basket carried by the woman in the foreground reveals that this picture was also painted during Gauguin's stay in the French colony of Martinique. The novelty of this canvas lies in its "exotic" subject matter – Caribbean women gathering fruit, whose clothing and turbans denote their African origin. The subject matter in this canvas is vastly removed from that favored by his Parisian contemporaries: city life, the theater, cafés and the crowds on the boulevards. If the technique is still the one learned in Paris, the subject matter reveals Gauguin's firm intention to distance himself from the modern world and to embrace what he believes to be the simplicity and purity of more primitive societies. He already had made an attempt to do this during a visit to Brittany in 1886. (He would return to Brittany several times before finally moving to

Tahiti.) Brittany, however, was not able to offer him the intense light of the tropics. And if there is one difference between this painting and the *Four Breton Women*, it is to be found in the quality of light, which falls strongly on the seated figure, thus modeling her form.

Under the Mangoes
1887, oil on canvas,
35 x 45½ in.
(89 x 116 cm.)
Van Gogh Museum,
Amsterdam

Vision After the Sermon is characterized by strong lines and unnatural coloring, combined with decorative elements such as the women's large white Breton bonnets

Cloisonnisme

"Cloison" in French means "separation" or "enclosure." "Cloissonnisme," therefore, refers to the technique of separating figurative elements by using a strong contour. The development of this pictorial language led to a style of painting without modeling or shadows, based on simple forms surrounded by dark lines and filled by areas of color. Referred to as both "cloissonisme" and "synthesism," Bernard was a particular follower of the trend, which drew its inspiration from Japanese prints, medieval stained glass and cloisonné enamels.

Vision After the Sermon

This work, marking an important stage in the artist's career, was painted during Gauguin's second stay in Pont-Aven, in 1888. During his stay, he met the young artist Emile Bernard, whose painting *Breton Women in the Fields* showed figures enclosed by thick outlines, very much in the style of a stained-glass window. This gave Gauguin the idea for his *Vision After the Sermon*, in which color is used in a completely unrealistic way and where the Impressionist technique gives way to flat areas of uniform color divided by clear outlines. Thus cloisonnisme came into being and Gauguin finally succeeded in making an intensely symbolic painting. This canvas, divided diagonally in two by the tree-trunk, shows the Old Testament scene of Jacob wrestling with the Angel, in the vision of the Breton women after mass. The simplicity of the design focuses one's

attention on the left foreground. The white caps, the intense red of the field where the wrestling is taking place and the simplified, "primitive" design, all combine to give this painting an air of intense expectancy. The painter's attempt to portray Breton religiosity has fully succeeded.

Vision After the Sermon
1888, oil on canvas, 28½ x 36 in.
(73 x 92 cm.)
National Gallery of Scotland, Edinburgh.

Self Portrait (Les Misérables)

Early in 1888, Vincent van Gogh left Paris for the south of France. He set up home in Arles and dreamed of founding an artists' colony. Gauguin did not seem particularly attracted to the idea and kept putting off his departure to join his friend. They did write letters to each other, full of accounts of their artistic experiments. It was during this period that van Gogh asked his friends Bernard and Gauguin for self-portraits, according to a practice common among artists of the time. Gauguin sent him his *Self Portrait (Les Misérables)*, which he described in the following way in a letter to Schuffenecker: "I think it is one of my best things: absolutely incomprehensible (for example), so abstract is it. In the first place the head is of a bandit called Jean Valjean [a character in Victor Hugo's *Les Misérables*]... The design is quite special, total abstraction. The eyes, mouth and nose are like flowers on a Persian carpet personifying the symbolic aspect. The color is a color remote from nature." In the background of this self portrait, Gauguin includes a painting of his friend Bernard as a symbol of their association. In Gauguin's terms, "total abstraction" means distancing oneself from nature and the independence of the image from visible reality.

les misérables
à mon Vincent
P Gauguin 88

**Self Portrait
(Les Misérables)**
1888, oil on canvas, 17¹/₂ x 21¹/₂
in. (45 x 55 cm.)
Van Gogh Museum, Amsterdam

Arlésiennes (Mistral)

With the financial help of Theo van Gogh, who ran an art gallery in Paris, Gauguin finally reached Arles in October 1888 and stayed there until December. In this period, he and van Gogh, in a spirit of rivalry, often painted the same subjects. Although the hospital of Arles and its garden are best known from the pictures van Gogh painted after his various stays there as a patient in 1889, Gauguin had already addressed this subject, most likely in December, 1888 while van Gogh was painting the park of Les Alycamps and its archeological finds. Rather than the garden itself, what Gauguin's canvas shows is the women of Arles wrapped in their cloaks, taking the air. As in *Vision After the Sermon*, the image is composed of large areas of concentrated and uniform color, which destroy any sense of spatial depth. Van Gogh's proximity may have been responsible for Gauguin's more explicit use of contrast between complementary colors, such as red and green and ocher and blue. In any case, despite the brilliance of the colors used, it is the dark cloaks of the women that are the key element in the painting, making

the atmosphere of the garden gloomy and tense. Gauguin's symbolism, arising from the arbitrary use of both color and shape, works to render the invisible visible.

Arlesiennes (Mistral)
1888, oil on canvas, 281/4 x 36 in.
(72 x 92 cm.)
The Art Institute of Chicago

IN THESE YEARS

1887–88 At this time the names of Gauguin and van Gogh were often linked and not because they worked together in Arles, but because they both moved beyond Impressionism and its study of light and began to give full value to color and line. Although emotionally very different, they were allied in their attitude toward color and revelled in its expressive power.

Night Café in the Place Lamartine

In September 1888, van Gogh painted the *Night Café in the Place Lamartine (in Arles)* showing a half-empty saloon with a billiards table in the middle and the last few clients scattered at the marble-topped tables. The atmosphere is made heavy by red walls and is further distorted by the halos of vibrant yellow light around the lamps hanging from the ceiling. This picture was an important precedent for Gauguin's *Night Café in Arles*. In it we see the same billiards table and the same red walls. Along with the figure in the foreground – Madame Ginoux, the café proprietor's wife – Gauguin has included some other typically van Gogh-like characters in the background: the Zouave on the left, for example, and the postman,

**Vincent van Gogh
L'Arlesienne,
Portrait of Madame
Ginoux**
1888, oil on canvas,
36¹/₂ x 29 in.
(93 x 74 cm.)
Musée d'Orsay, Paris

**Vincent van Gogh
Night Café in the
Place Lamartine**
1888, oil on canvas,
27¹/₂ x 35 in.
(70 x 89 cm.)
*Yale University Art
Gallery, New Haven*

After a period of joint creativity, their strong personalities came into conflict and culminated in a violent scene where van Gogh, according to Gauguin, went quite mad and threatened him with a razor. Van Gogh then turned the razor on himself and cut off his own ear.

Night Café in Arles
1888, oil on canvas,
28¼ x 36 in.
(72 x 92 cm.)
*Puskin Museum,
Moscow*

Joseph Roulin, on the right. By focusing the viewer's attention on the figure of the woman, who establishes a rapport with the observer by her gaze and her smile, Gauguin attenuates the tension that pervades his friend's picture. This is an example of the intense exchange between the two painters during their Provençal period, when they tended to control each other's work. The portrait of *L'Arlesienne (Woman of Arles)* or *Portrait of Madame Ginoux*, of which van Gogh painted more than one version, derives, for example, from a drawing by Gauguin.

1888 After leaving Arles, Gauguin returned to Paris and then moved on to Pont-Aven and the nearby village of Le Pouldu. He worked closely with, and was the leading figure in, a group of figures who became known as the "Pont-Aven School," a group of artists that included Bernard, Laval and Sérusier.

1889 To coincide with the Exposition Universelle the Pont-Aven painters exhibited their works at the Café Volpini calling themselves "synthétistes." Gauguin made friends with Charles Morice, Octave Mirbeau, Stéphane Mallarmé and Albert Aurier at this time.

Bonjour Monsieur Gauguin
1889, oil on canvas,
44¹/₂ x 36 in. (113 x 92 cm.)
Narodne Gallerie, Prague

Bonjour, Monsieur Gauguin

When, in 1889, the artist painted *Bonjour, Monsieur Gauguin*, he was once again in Brittany. The painting's subject matter – a meeting during a walk in the country – as the title suggests, was a reference to Gustave Courbet's meeting, known as *Bonjour, Monsieur Courbet*, of 1854. As the critics have noted, the central theme in Courbet's work is the artist's need to exist outside of social restrictions or conventions; clearly a romantic dream. This theme, however, couples perfectly with Gauguin's own yearnings for freedom and his dream of losing himself in distant lands. However, while his predecessor's painting was largely realistic, Gauguin's version is tinted with the fantastic: the colors are very intense; the branches of the trees have almost become arabesques over a background which is more fantastical than realistic. Even the figure of the painter, who is walking toward us wrapped in a heavy cloak, has been strongly simplified. Writing from Brittany, Gauguin said: "I find something wild and primitive in it. When my clogs resound on this granite soil, I hear a dumb, opaque and powerful tone that I look for in the painting." Gauguin's incessant experimentation is underlined by the fact that his paintings of this period show a return to the short, parallel brushstrokes that he used before his trip to Arles.

GAUGUIN IN BRITTANY
Gauguin made six trips to Brittany. The Pont-Aven area was known to painters for its ongoing and deep-rooted folk traditions and for the low cost of living. Gauguin went there first in 1886 and returned in 1888 when, after his encounter with Emile Bernard, he adopted cloisonnisme. He was back again in 1889, in the winter of 1889–90 and again the following summer when he also stayed at Le Pouldu. His last visit was in 1894, just before his final departure for the Pacific Islands.

La Belle Angèle

This painting was commissioned as a portrait of Madame Satre, the wife of the future mayor of Pont-Aven. According to a letter from Theo van Gogh to his brother Vincent, the painting was rejected by the model. This canvas encapsulates all of the experiments Gauguin had conducted up until its painting: the arbitrary, subjective use of color; the attempt to free himself from the confines of external, visible reality; the parallel brushstrokes taken from Cézanne's work; the decentralized composition taken from Japanese prints; the inclusion of traditional cultural elements, such as clothing, religious symbols, or objects from so-called primitive cultures; and, finally, the almost total absence of spatial depth. By placing the portrait of the woman from Breton next to the tiny statue of an Incan idol — an association between two very distinct cultures — Gauguin seems to announce his imminent departure for distant lands. The statue is also a reference to Gauguin's Peruvian childhood, which may have influenced his desire to live far from the cosmopolitan and, in his view, corrupt city of Paris.

La Belle Angèle
1889, oil on canvas,
36 x 28$\frac{1}{2}$ in. (92 x 73 cm.)
Musée d'Orsay, Paris

Gauguin's model for the Awakening *was a young Parisienne woman (and the artist's lover for a time), called Juliette Huette.*

Awakening of Spring

Gauguin spent the winter of 1890–91 in Paris. Two paintings of female nudes can be dated to this time. These are a copy of Manet's *Olympia* and the *Awakening of Spring*, also known as *The Loss of Virginity*. The study after Manet and the picture reproduced here seem to presage what will, from this time on, be a recurrent theme in Gauguin's work. A short time later, Gauguin arrives in Tahiti, and once he has gained the confidence of the locals, he has no difficulty finding female models to pose naked for him. The *Awakening of Spring* contains a number of symbols: the fox perching on the nubile girl is a symbol of perversity – it already had appeared with

the same meaning in his bas-relief *Love, And You Will Be Happy*, while the cyclamen that the young woman holds in her hand represents her recent deflowering. The pale

figure stands out very strongly against the simplified and predominantly dark landscape. In this, Gauguin emulates Manet's *Olympia*, in which an extremely white nude emerges from a dark background.

Awakening of Spring
1890, oil on canvas,
35^1/$_4$ x 40^1/$_2$ in.
(90 x 103 cm.)
*The Chrysler Museum,
Norfolk, Virginia*

25

Vahine No Te Tiare (Woman With A Flower)

It may have been the wife of the painter Odilon Redon, herself born on Réunion, who suggested to Gauguin that he go to Tahiti. After a lengthy sea voyage with stops in Bombay, Melbourne, Sydney and Numea, the painter finally arrived on June 8, 1891 at Papeete, the island where he hoped to find the simplicity that he so desired and that Paris had been unable to supply. He even managed to attain a position in the Ministry of Education and Fine Arts. The first pictures he painted in Tahiti were not much different from the ones he had done previously in Brittany and Paris. This is the case with *Vahine No Te Tiare*, where the principal novelty is the model with her marked Polynesian features. The composition and use of color, on the other hand, are those of his European works (and the works of his colleagues). The flowers in the background, for example, which have no symbolic significance here, recall both his *Self Portrait (Les Misérables)* and his *Belle Angèle*. The division of the background into two fields of uniform color – one yellow, the other red – recalls not only the backgrounds of many of van Gogh's portraits (such as the *Portrait of Camille Roulin*, or the *Self Portrait with Bandaged Ear and Pipe*), but also Gauguin's own *Self Portrait with Halo*. Nevertheless, there is a new and evident monumentality to *Vahine No Te Tiare*.

Vahine No Te Tiare (Woman With A Flower)
1891, oil on canvas, 27 1/2 x 18 in. (70 x 46 cm.), *Ny Carlsberg Glypotek, Copenhagen*

Two Women on the Beach

This is one of the few works Gauguin produced in Tahiti in 1891. Although the background, with its band of color, is still reminiscent of his European work, we already can see, in the pose of the two seated women, the results of Gauguin's careful studies of the people on the island, their customs and bearing. The two women are depicted in the most natural and relaxed of poses, creating an almost sleepy effect. Their forms are enclosed by thick outlines and warm colors predominate – creating the impression of a hot summer's afternoon. Gauguin tried to explain the significance of his Tahitian experience in these terms: "It is an open-air life, yet intimate, among shady streams, with the woman chattering as in an immense palace decorated by nature, with all the riches that Tahiti possesses. This is what provides all those marvellous colors, that sweltering, yet tranquil, silent air." *Two Women on the Beach* is the first example of a style of painting that will reappear in much of Gauguin's later work.

Two Women on the Beach
1891, oil on canvas, 27 x 36 in. (69 x 92 cm.) Musée d'Orsay, Paris

Aha Oe Feii (Are You Jealous?)

As with *Two Women on the Beach*, Gauguin has chosen to show two women together in a relaxed and confidential atmosphere. The virtually abstract background does not allow us to say with certainty whether the scene is on the beach. The two nudes are more sculptured and they lend a greater sense of spatial depth to the composition. Although their positions seem spontaneous, the pose of the woman seated in the central part of the painting derives from a classical sculpture of Dionysus, of which Gauguin owned a photograph. It shows us that, even in Tahiti, Gauguin had not entirely forgotten his European roots. On the contrary, he deliberately sought out points of contact between ancient Mediterranean culture and what he saw in Polynesia.

This painting belongs to Gauguin's early Tahitian period and is a perfect example of his synthetic style applied to exotic new subjects.

Aha Oe Feii (Are You Jealous?) 1892,
oil on canvas,
26 x 35 in. (66 x 89 cm.)
Puskin Museum, Moscow

1891 From June on, Gauguin lives in the Tahitian capital, Papeete. However, bad relations with the local authorities and a shortage of funds force him to return to Paris, where he arrives in the summer of 1893.

The artist comes into an inheritance of 9,000 francs. This allows him a period of financial security.

Ta Matete
(The Market)

Despite the title, the painting concentrates not on the market in Papeete but on the women who go there. Gauguin tries to establish a rapport between the Tahitian women and the monumental figures in ancient Egyptian bas-reliefs and murals. In fact, among the numerous reproductions he took with him to Tahiti was a photograph of a mural painting discovered in a tomb in Thebes, which now resides in the British Museum. The women in the painting are arranged as if in a frieze, and – exactly as in the Egyptian mural – they are shown with their upper bodies turned frontally, and their legs and heads in profile (except

Detail from a banqueting scene, from a New Kingdom tomb in ancient Egypt.

TA MATETE

for the central figure). Here, and elsewhere, the artist delves ever more deeply into the questions of color, intensity of light and the

locals' way of life. At the same time, he makes strong references to other cultures, especially ancient ones.

**Ta Matete
(The Market)**
1892, oil on canvas,
28$^1/_2$ x 36 in.
(73 x 91.5 cm.)
Kunstmuseum, Basel

IN THESE YEARS

1893 Gauguin stays in France for two years, but is very disillusioned by the lack of critical and public success of his Tahitian paintings. **1895** He leaves France for the last time to return to Tahiti.

Ea Haere Ia Oe (Where Are You Going?)

The young woman we see in the foreground is most probably Teha'amana, a thirteen-year-old Tahitian girl whom Gauguin had married in 1892, with the permission of her parents, and who lived with him in his cabin at Mataiea, some twenty-five miles from Papeete. Some say that Gauguin married her exclusively for artistic reasons, so that he could use her as a model whenever he wanted. Gauguin already had a wife and children in Europe, as well as a mistress who bore him a child after he left for Tahiti. Furthermore, he was on the verge of leaving the island. With its joyful colors, we find all the ingredients of Gauguin's art in this painting: *cloisonnisme*; a subjective, non-realistic use of color; references to the simplicity of so-called primitive society; and a striking naturalness to his models.

The Tahitian women's poses, like the one shown in the detail above, become a leit-motif in Gauguin's paintings. He does not hesitate to fix them in canonical positions and to use them again and again.

Ea Haere Ia Oe (Where Are You Going?)
1893, oil on canvas, 28½ x 36 in. (73 x 91.5 cm.)
Kunstmuseum, Basel

IN THESE YEARS

1895 Gauguin returns to Tahiti where he spends most of his time in a hut, ill and impoverished.

1897 Gauguin attempts suicide. "I believe that everything that should and should not have been said about me has already been said. All I now want is silence, silence and more silence. Let me die in peace, forgotten."

Where Do We Come From? What Are We? Where Are We Going?

In 1897, Gauguin found himself in moral, physical and financial difficulties. The paradise he had been painting and describing had become a disappointment to him. Although he had found a simpler, more "primitive" and spontaneous society in French Polynesia, the civilization he sought to escape had arrived in these islands long before him. The Polynesian people, besieged by Christian missionaries, had already been introduced to the social and industrial models of the modern world. To make matters worse, his work was incomprehensible to most people in Europe. All of this induced him to attempt

suicide, but not before painting what was to be regarded as a pictorial last will and testament – the painting was *Where Do We Come From? What Are We? Where Are We Going?* This work is a panel the size of a fresco filled with complex symbolism. The painting unfolds, from right to left, as an allegory of life in a paradise of simplicity and virginal nature. The allegory begins with the new-born baby, at lower right, and concludes with the figure of a dying old woman, at lower left. But as Gauguin himself puts it: "Two sinister figures [in the background] next to the tree of knowledge add a note of anguish which is caused by the relationship knowledge has with simple beings." With sadness, Gauguin acknowledges the end of a dream.

Where Do We Come From? What Are We? Where Are We Going?
1897, oil on canvas, 54³/₄ x 147¹/₂ in. (139 x 375 cm.) *Museum of Fine Arts, Boston*

1900 In January, the artist signs a contract with the Parisian art dealer, Vollard, that will guarantee him a regular income.

1901 Gauguin decides to move, together with Tehura and their child, to the island of Hiva Oa on the Marquesas archipelago. He continues the struggle, begun in Papeete, for the rights of the indigenous people of the islands, in opposition to Catholic missions and the colonial administration. This lands him in prison for three months. Although his health is rapidly deteriorating, he paints until the end.

1903 Gauguin dies on May 8 after two heart attacks. The locals shout: "Gauguin is dead and we are lost!" The bishop of the Martin Catholic Mission destroys the artists' paintings on the grounds that they are both licentious and profane.

Riders on the Beach

This is one of Gauguin's last paintings. The fact that he had not previously tackled the subject of horses in motion is somewhat surprising. Horse-racing was one of the favorite subjects of Degas, who was a constant point of reference for Gauguin. This was clearly a way of paying homage to his friend and indirect master. What is surprising is the mysterious, as opposed to the symbolic, character of this painting. Three black or bay horses with their darkly attired riders advance toward the sea. They are almost certainly natives of the Marquesas Isles, where Gauguin had been living since 1901 and where he was to die. Their way is about to be barred by two grey horses ridden by figures in circus costumes – one red and one yellow. The scene is disturbing, even though it is not quite clear what is happening. Perhaps it is in this work that we discern the limitation of Gauguin's painting, splendid and suggestive as it is. Without the help of the artist's annotations or his letters to friends – in which he frequently explains his paintings – the meaning of many of his works would remain obscure.

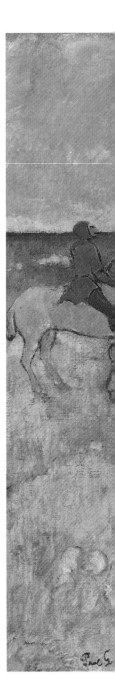

Riders on the Beach
1902, oil on canvas,
$25^1/_2$ x $29^3/_4$ in. (65.5 x 75.9 cm.)
Folkwang Museum, Essen

Index of Gauguin's works:

*The numbers in bold refer to pages where the work is reproduced.

First American edition published in 2003 by
Enchanted Lion Books
115 West 18th Street,New York, NY 10011
Copyright © 2002 McRae Books Srl
English language text copyright © 2003 McRae Books Srl
All rights reserved
Printed and bound in the Slovak Republic

Library of Congress Cataloging-in-Publication Data
Siponta De Salvia, Maria.
  Paul Gauguin / Maria Siponta De Salvia.—1st American ed.
    p. cm. — (Great artists)
  Includes index.
  Summary: Discusses the style and technique of the French Impressionist painter Paul Gauguin.
  ISBN 1-59270-010-1
    1. Gauguin, Paul, 1848-1903—Criticism and interpretation—Juvenile literature. [1 Gauguin, Paul, 1848-1903. 2. Artists. 3. Painting, French.] I. Gauguin, Paul, 1848-1903. II. Title. III. Great artists (Enchanted Lion Books)
ND553.G27S5 2003   2003049056
759.4—dc21
The series "Great Artists" was created and produced by
McRae Books Srl, Borgo Santa Croce, 8, Florence, Italy
Info@mcraebooks.com
Series editor: Roberto Carvalho de Magalhães
Text: Maria Siponta de Salvia
Design: Marco Nardi / Layouts: Laura Ottina
The Publishers would like to thank the following museums and archives
who have authorized the reproduction of the works in this book: The Bridgeman Art Library,
London (9, 34); Scala Group, Florence (Cover, 1, 3, 4-5, 6-7, 10, 11, 13, 15, 16-17, 18, 21, 22-23, 24, 25, 26, 27, 28, 29, 30, 31, 33, 35, 37, 39).

Cover: **When Do You Marry?**, 1892, (detail)
Page 1: **Self Portrait (Les Miserables),** l888 (detail)